Jane Addams

by

Melanie Zucker Stanley

FOXHOUND PUBLISHING, LLC

Glen Allen, Virginia

Thanks to my husband, Tim, and various friends
for reading the manuscript.

Foxhound Publishing, LLC
P.O. Box 5543
Glen Allen, Virginia
www.foxhoundpublishing.com

An Editorial Directions Book

Library of Congress
Card Catalog Number: 00-106760

Printed in the United States of America

Contents

Who Was Jane Addams?

Jane Addams was a friend to the poor. She helped poor children and their families. She worked hard to help them have a better life. Jane's work with the poor began at a place called Hull House.

Read this book to learn the story of Jane Addams.

Jane Addams helped poor families. ▶

Hard Lives

One day, a little girl was out walking with her father. Suddenly she stopped and stared. She saw dirty, run-down houses everywhere. They were nothing like the nice house she lived in. "Daddy, daddy!" the little girl cried. "Why do people live in such awful little houses?" Her father said, "The people who live here are very poor."

The little girl wanted to help them. She said, "Someday I will live in a poor neighborhood like this." That little girl was Jane Addams.

◀ Young Jane saw the hard lives of the poor children around her.

Jane's Early Life

Jane Addams was born in Cedarville, Illinois, on September 6, 1860. When Jane was two years old, her mother died. Jane's older sisters and brother helped her father take care of her.

John Addams was Jane's father. He loved Jane very much. He taught her to work hard, do her best, and be fair to others. He told her to think for herself.

Jane was sick a lot when she was growing up. She walked with her toes turned in and her back was not straight. Jane did not let this stop her though. She had fun with her family and she did her best in school.

One day Jane Addams would grow up and ▶ do all that she promised.

8

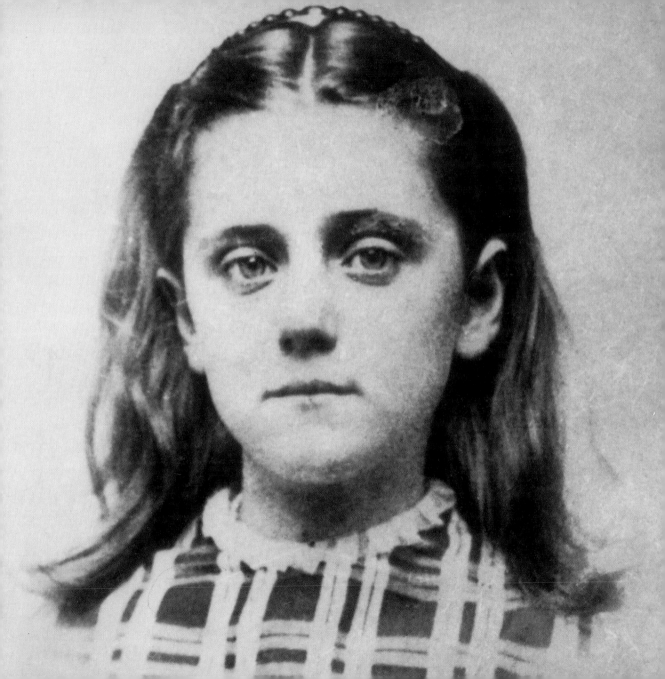

When Jane was seventeen she went to college. At college, she met a new friend named Ellen Starr. Jane told Ellen she wanted to do something useful with her life. But Jane was not sure what she could do.

Most girls did not go to college in those days, but Jane had a mind of her own. Jane and Ellen went to Europe after college. Jane saw something in Europe that gave her a wonderful idea. She saw a settlement house.

A settlement house was a place where poor people could go for help. The people who ran the settlement house worked to help poor people live a better life.

◄ Jane wanted to do something useful with her life.

Helping the Poor

Now Jane knew how she could be useful. She could help the poor. She could start a settlement house in America.

Jane knew it was going to be hard work. She asked her friend Ellen Starr to help. Jane and Ellen went to Chicago, Illinois, to open a settlement house.

Ellen Starr helped Jane open a settlement ▶ house.

Immigrants in Chicago

At that time, most of the people in Chicago were immigrants. Immigrants are people who come to America from other countries. Jane wanted to help the newcomers in Chicago.

Immigrants had a hard life in Chicago. They did not speak much English. They worked long hours for very little money. Even their little children had to work. Immigrant families were very, very poor.

◀ Many immigrant families came to Chicago without much money.

Hull House

Jane found a big house. The house was in a run-down immigrant area. Jane named it Hull House. Jane made Hull House one of the first settlement houses in America.

Jane loved helping children. She opened a day-care center and a kindergarten at Hull House. Later, Jane helped to open the first playground in Chicago.

Jane named her settlement house Hull House. ▶

A Big School

Jane helped the grown-ups too. She helped them find better jobs. She opened a library and helped them learn to read, write, and speak English. In some ways, Hull House was like a big school.

Hull House was a very busy place, and Jane was a very busy woman. In the first year of Hull House, 50,000 people came to find help!

◀ Grown-ups came to Hull House to learn reading and many other skills.

The Children

In those days, many children worked long hours. They had to work in places that were not safe. Many children worked in factories. Factories had machines that were unsafe for children.

Jane hated to see children work so hard. There were no laws to help these children. Jane worked hard to change that. She helped to make new labor laws that would help children. Jane worked hard to get labor laws passed that were fair to children. She also wanted cleaner streets and better homes.

Young children worked all day in factories ▶ and mills.

Jane's Last Years

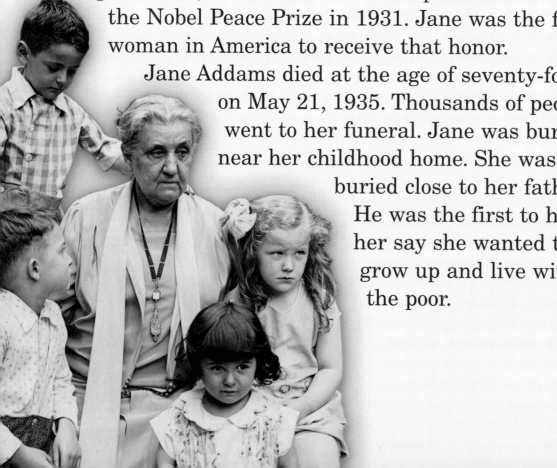

All her life, Jane worked to help others. As she grew older, she worked for world peace. She won the Nobel Peace Prize in 1931. Jane was the first woman in America to receive that honor.

Jane Addams died at the age of seventy-four on May 21, 1935. Thousands of people went to her funeral. Jane was buried near her childhood home. She was buried close to her father. He was the first to hear her say she wanted to grow up and live with the poor.

Remember These Dates for Jane Addams

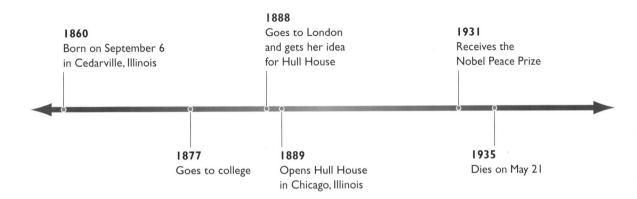

1860
Born on September 6
in Cedarville, Illinois

1888
Goes to London
and gets her idea
for Hull House

1931
Receives the
Nobel Peace Prize

1877
Goes to college

1889
Opens Hull House
in Chicago, Illinois

1935
Dies on May 21

Spend More Time with Jane Addams

Reading

Simon, Charnan. *Jane Addams: Pioneer
Social Worker.* Danbury, Conn.:
Children's Press, 1997.
Wheeler, Leslie A. *Jane Addams:
Pioneers in Change.* Englewood Cliffs,
N.J.: Silver Burdett Press, 1990.

Online

**Jane Addams Hull House Museum
Home Page**
*http://www.uic.edu/jaddams/hull/
hull_house.html*
For a timeline of Jane Addams's life
and successes at Hull House

Index

Photo Credits

Photographs ©
AP/Wide World: 10; Archive Photos: 21; Corbis: cover, 6, 14; Corbis/Bettmann: 17, 18; Corbis/Underwood & Underwood: 5, 22; Jack Zucker: 24; University of Illinois at Chicago, The University Library (Jane Addams Memorial Collection): 9, 13.

About the Author

Melanie Zucker Stanley works as a social studies curriculum teacher for Fairfax County, Virginia, developing materials for teachers and children. She also works as a freelance writer, storyteller, and photographer. Her passion is history, and she enjoys bringing history to life for children. Melanie Zucker Stanley lives with her husband, Tim, and two children, Aaron and Melanie, in Herndon, Virginia.